CIVIL RIGHTS HEROES

Martin Luther King Jr.

By Amy B. Rogers

New York

Published in 2022 by Cavendish Square Publishing, LLC
29 E. 21st Street, New York, NY 10010

Copyright © 2022 by Cavendish Square Publishing, LLC

First Edition

No part of this publication may be reproduced, stored in a retrieval system, or transmitted in any form or by any means—electronic, mechanical, photocopying, recording, or otherwise—without the prior permission of the copyright owner. Request for permission should be addressed to Permissions, Cavendish Square Publishing, 243 5th Avenue, Suite 136, New York, NY 10016. Tel (877) 980-4450; fax (877) 980-4454.

Website: cavendishsq.com

This publication represents the opinions and views of the author based on his or her personal experience, knowledge, and research. The information in this book serves as a general guide only. The author and publisher have used their best efforts in preparing this book and disclaim liability rising directly or indirectly from the use and application of this book.

All websites were available and accurate when this book was sent to press.

Portions of this work were originally authored by Barbara M. Linde and published as *Martin Luther King Jr. (Civil Rights Crusaders)*.
All new material this edition authored by Amy B. Rogers.

Library of Congress Cataloging-in-Publication Data

Names: Rogers, Amy B., author.
Title: Martin Luther King Jr. / Amy B. Rogers.
Description: New York : Cavendish Square Publishing, [2022] | Series: The inside guide: Civil Rights heroes | Includes bibliographical references and index.
Identifiers: LCCN 2020027780 | ISBN 9781502660084 (library binding) | ISBN 9781502660060 (paperback) | ISBN 9781502660077 (set) | ISBN 9781502660091 (ebook)
Subjects: LCSH: King, Martin Luther, Jr., 1929-1968–Juvenile literature. | African American civil rights workers–Biography–Juvenile literature. | Civil rights–United States–History–Juvenile literature
Classification: LCC E185.97.K5 R585 2022 | DDC 323.092 [B]–dc23
LC record available at https://lccn.loc.gov/2020027780

Editor: Katie Kawa
Copy Editor: Abby Young
Designer: Andrea Davison-Bartolotta

The photographs in this book are used by permission and through the courtesy of: Cover Consolidated News Pictures/Hulton Archive/Getty Images; pp. 4, 7, 20, 23, 28 (bottom right) Bettmann/Getty Images; p. 6 Pgiam/iStock Unreleased/Getty Images; p. 8 Raymond Boyd/Getty Images; p. 9 Olivier Douliery/AFP via Getty Images; p. 10 Donald Uhrbrock/The LIFE Images Collection via Getty Images/Getty Images; p. 12 Al Pucci/NY Daily News Archive via Getty Images; p. 13 Photo12/UIG/Getty Images; pp. 14, 29 (top) Don Cravens/The LIFE Images Collection via Getty Images/Getty Images; pp. 15, 22 Mario Tama/Getty Images; p. 16 Ernst Haas/Hulton Archive/Getty Images; p. 18 Michael Ochs Archives/Getty Images; p. 19 Paul Schutzer/The LIFE Picture Collection via Getty Images; p. 21 Okamoto/PhotoQuest/Getty Images; p. 24 Santi Visalli/Archive Photos/Getty Images; p. 25 Brooks Kraft LLC/Corbis Historical/Getty Images; p. 26 Sean Gardner/Getty Images; p. 27 Ira L. Black/Corbis News/Getty Images; p. 28 (top left) Robert W. Kelley/The LIFE Picture Collection via Getty Images; p. 28 (bottom left) Afro American Newspapers/Gado/Getty Images; p. 28 (top right) Hulton Archive/Getty Images; p. 29 (bottom) Stefano Guidi/Getty Images.

Some of the images in this book illustrate individuals who are models. The depictions do not imply actual situations or events.

CPSIA compliance information: Batch #CS22CSQ: For further information contact Cavendish Square Publishing LLC, New York, New York, at 1-877-980-4450.

Printed in the United States of America

CONTENTS

Chapter One   5
    "I Have a Dream"

Chapter Two   11
    A Leader's First Steps

Chapter Three   17
    Major Moments

Chapter Four   23
    A Legacy of Leadership

Timeline   28

Think About It!   29

Glossary   30

Find Out More   31

Index   32

Dr. Martin Luther King Jr. gave his "I Have a Dream" speech in 1963 in Washington, D.C. It's still considered one of the most well-known speeches in American history.

"I HAVE A DREAM"

Chapter One

The civil rights movement was one of the most important events in the 20th century in the United States. In the 1950s and 1960s, big changes were made in the fight for equal rights for Black Americans, thanks to this movement. One of the most famous figures in the civil rights movement was Dr. Martin Luther King Jr. His words and actions still inspire people in the United States—and around the world—today.

Fast Fact

Martin studied religion in college. He earned his doctorate—the highest college degree a person can receive—from Boston University in Massachusetts in 1955. This is why he's known as Dr. Martin Luther King Jr.

A Celebrated Speaker

Martin Luther King Jr. is known for his powerful speeches about civil rights. His words helped change the world!

Martin's most famous speech is known today as his "I Have a Dream" speech. He delivered it at the March on Washington for Jobs and Freedom in Washington, D.C., on August 28, 1963. In this speech, he said, "I have a dream that my four little children will one day live in a nation where they will not be judged by the color of their skin but by the content of their character." Martin dreamed of a better world for his children, and he worked hard to try to build that world by fighting back against racism in the United States.

Fast Fact
Martin's four children were named Yolanda, Martin III, Dexter, and Bernice.

This marker shows the place where Martin delivered his "I Have a Dream" speech.

WHAT'S RACISM?

Leaders of the civil rights movement, including Martin Luther King Jr., called attention to the problem of racism in the United States. Racism is a belief that one race is better than others. In a racist system, that race is treated better than others. In the United States, white people have always been in power, so racism in this country is directed toward Black Americans and other people of color.

Black Americans have often faced discrimination, which is unfair and unequal treatment. For many years, they also faced segregation, which was the forced separation of people of different races. The civil rights movement led to the end of legal segregation.

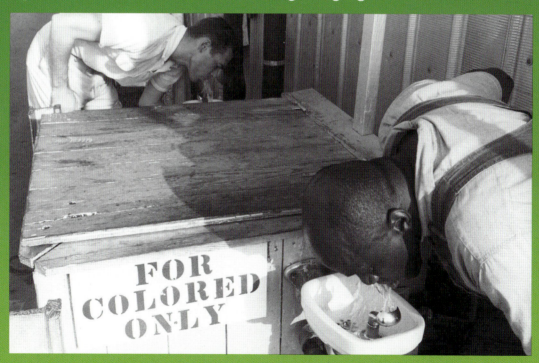

Many parts of the United States had laws that enforced segregation for many years. Black Americans had separate schools, restaurants, and even water fountains. Often, these facilities for Black Americans were much worse than those white Americans were able to use.

Gone Too Soon

Martin's dream lived on after his death. He was assassinated, or murdered, on April 4, 1968. Martin's death made people across the United States sad and angry, but they didn't give up. They kept working to fight for civil rights.

Martin's wife, Coretta Scott King, worked hard to keep his memory alive. She was a big part of the civil rights movement too. She started what's known as the King Center the year he died to honor his **legacy** by continuing to educate people about the fight against racism. People can still visit the King Center to learn about Martin and his work.

Still Fighting

Martin Luther King Jr.'s words and work are just as important today as they were in the 1950s and 1960s. People across the United States

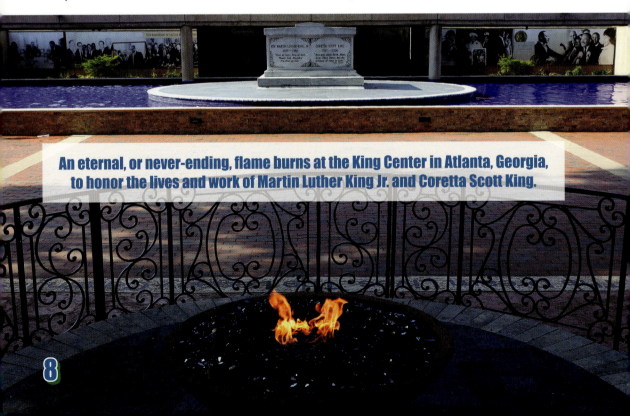

An eternal, or never-ending, flame burns at the King Center in Atlanta, Georgia, to honor the lives and work of Martin Luther King Jr. and Coretta Scott King.

are still fighting against racism and to make sure Black Americans are treated fairly and equally.

In 2020, protests and marches were held in all 50 U.S. states and around the world to call attention to the racism that still exists in the United States. The leaders of these protests followed in the footsteps of those who came before them, including Martin Luther King Jr. By learning about his story and the time in which he lived, we can learn how to use our voices to continue to call for change in the world around us.

Fast Fact

In 1986, the United States began celebrating a national holiday to honor Martin Luther King Jr. This holiday is celebrated on the third Monday of January every year.

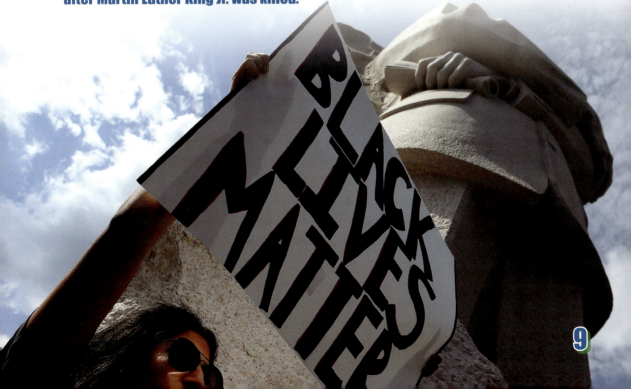

The Black Lives Matter movement of the 21st century has its roots in the civil rights movement. Black Americans are still fighting for their rights more than 50 years after Martin Luther King Jr. was killed.

Martin came from a long line of Baptist preachers. His father and grandfather were both pastors at the Ebenezer Baptist Church in Atlanta, and Martin also preached at this church.

A LEADER'S FIRST STEPS

Chapter Two

Martin Luther King Jr. was born in Atlanta, Georgia, on January 15, 1929. He grew up in the segregated South, and he experienced racism and discrimination in many parts of his everyday life. As Martin grew up and developed his leadership skills, he began working to end segregation and fight for equal rights for Black Americans.

A Man of Faith

Martin followed in the footsteps of both his father and grandfather, who were Baptist preachers. Both men went to Morehouse College, and Martin started school there in 1944, when he was only 15 years old.

After Martin graduated from Morehouse in 1948, he continued his studies in Pennsylvania and later in Boston. While he was in Boston, he met Coretta Scott. Martin and Coretta got married in 1953.

Fast Fact

Martin was born with the first name Michael, which was also his father's name. His father later changed both their names to Martin Luther. This honored an important German minister from the 1500s with that name.

The next year, Martin began serving as the pastor of a church in Montgomery, Alabama. This was where his work as a civil rights hero would begin.

Coretta Scott King was much more than just Martin's wife. She was a leader in her own right and a talented musician who studied singing and violin.

Boycotting Buses

Even buses were segregated in the South in the 1950s. On December 1, 1955, a Black woman named Rosa Parks refused to give up her seat on the bus to a white man in Montgomery. She was arrested, but many people felt that was unfair. They wanted to fight back against the segregated bus system in Montgomery.

Groups that worked for racial equality planned a bus boycott in Montgomery. This meant people stopped taking city buses, and the city's bus system lost a lot of money.

Martin became a leader of the boycott. He helped organize it and acted as a **spokesperson** for the Black community in Montgomery. This was his first major leadership **role** in the civil rights movement.

Martin in the Spotlight

In a speech about the Montgomery bus boycott, Martin said, "We have no alternative but to protest." This meant he felt the only choice for Black people in Montgomery was to take action. These words inspired many people. However, other people, especially racist white Americans, didn't like what Martin was saying.

Rosa Parks stood up for her rights when she felt she was being treated unfairly. Her actions helped end the segregation of buses in Montgomery and around the country.

Fast Fact
The Montgomery bus boycott lasted for more than 380 days!

People tried to stop Martin by arresting him and even by throwing **dynamite** at his house. No one was hurt when this happened, but it showed how much danger Martin was in just for speaking his mind and wanting all people to be treated equally.

The Boycott Ends

After more than a year, the U.S. Supreme Court declared that it was unconstitutional, or against the U.S. Constitution, to segregate buses. The Montgomery bus boycott had been a success, and Martin was praised as its leader.

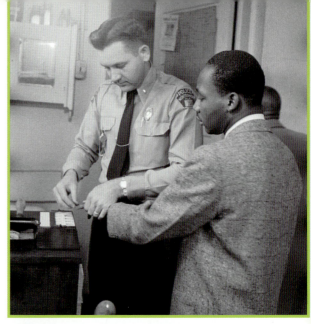

Martin Luther King Jr. was arrested for his actions during the Montgomery bus boycott. During his lifetime, he was arrested 29 times, but he didn't let this stop him from fighting for what he knew was right.

Martin's leadership of the boycott earned him a lot of respect among other Black leaders. In 1957, he helped create the Southern Christian Leadership Conference (SCLC) to support and help organize the civil rights movement. Martin served as president of this organization, which helped lead the movement into a new **era**. Martin's work with the SCLC helped him become one of the most famous faces of the civil rights movement.

Fast Fact

In 1958, Martin's book *Stride Toward Freedom: The Montgomery Story* was published. At a book signing that year, a woman stabbed Martin in the chest. He survived after a long surgery to fix the wound.

DIFFERENT WAYS TO PROTEST

Boycotts were an important kind of protest used during the civil rights movement. Another was sit-ins, in which Black people refused to leave counters where lunch was served to white people until they were served too. Marches also took place. All of these were considered nonviolent, or peaceful, forms of protest, which was the kind of protesting Martin most often supported.

However, in certain cases, Martin said he understood why some Black people chose to riot, or violently **disturb** the peace, as a form of protest. In Martin's words, "A riot is the language of the unheard." He believed people needed to look more closely at what would drive Black Americans to turn to violent forms of protest.

Many Black Americans today still feel unheard.

Martin's speeches were shared with the world through radio, newspapers, and television.

MAJOR MOMENTS

Chapter Three

While the 1950s marked the start of Martin's career as a civil rights leader, he reached the peak of his power in the 1960s. During this decade, his words and actions brought attention to the civil rights movement in a major way, especially through the relatively new medium of television.

In Prison in Birmingham

In 1963, Martin helped organize a campaign to fight segregation in Birmingham, Alabama. During this campaign, television cameras captured the violence that Black Americans fighting for civil rights experienced. The police in Birmingham used hoses and dogs to try to stop the protesters, but they kept going.

Martin was put in jail for his part in the Birmingham protests. While he was there, he wrote down his thoughts about the civil rights movement. "Letter from a Birmingham Jail" became one of the most famous pieces of writing created during the civil rights movement.

Fast Fact
Martin worked with many other civil rights leaders in Birmingham. They included Fred Shuttlesworth, who was the leader of the Alabama Christian Movement for Human Rights.

Martin can be seen here with Fred Shuttlesworth. Together, the two men helped lead a campaign in Birmingham that desegregated many parts of the city, including lunch counters and bathrooms.

The March on Washington

To continue the push for equality, which was gaining more attention after Birmingham, Martin helped organize a march in Washington, D.C. This became the March on Washington for Jobs and Freedom. More than 200,000 people took part in this march and heard Martin deliver his "I Have a Dream" speech in person.

The spirit of hope behind the march was captured by Martin when he said he dreamed of a world "where little Black boys and Black girls will be able to join hands with little white boys and white girls as sisters and brothers."

Fast Fact

Martin won the Nobel Peace Prize in 1964. This is a famous prize given to people who work for peace around the world.

The March on Washington showed the strength of the civil rights movement to the entire nation.

From Selma to Montgomery

Selma, Alabama, was the site of a major campaign in the 1960s to register, or sign up, Black people to vote. For many years, unfair laws had been in place to keep Black people from voting. Martin and other leaders wanted to fight those laws and help Black people vote.

Martin helped plan a march from Selma to Montgomery that would take place on March 7, 1965. Although Martin didn't take part in that march, many other civil rights leaders did. The marchers were met with violence, and it was so unsafe that they were forced to turn back to Selma.

Two days later, Martin helped lead marchers from Selma across the Edmund Pettus Bridge. They then stopped to pray and turned back. Finally, on March 21, another march set out from Selma that finally reached the state capital.

Fast Fact
March 7, 1965, became known as "Bloody Sunday" because of the violence the marchers from Selma faced.

Martin helped the marches from Selma to Montgomery gain a lot of attention. However, some other civil rights leaders didn't agree with his methods. They thought he should have kept going on March 9 instead of turning back.

IMPORTANT ACTS

The civil rights movement led to new laws that helped make the United States a fairer and more equal place. President Lyndon B. Johnson signed the Civil Rights Act of 1964 as Martin looked on. This act made discrimination in public places and in the workforce illegal. It also gave the U.S. government power to enforce laws to stop segregation in schools and other places.

The Voting Rights Act of 1965 was a direct result of the marches from Selma to Montgomery. This act made it illegal to discriminate against voters because of their race.

Martin met with President Lyndon B. Johnson to talk about important issues affecting the Black community in the United States.

The Martin Luther King, Jr. Memorial stands in Washington, D.C., as a reminder of the life and legacy of this civil rights hero.

A LEGACY OF LEADERSHIP

Chapter Four

Martin continued to fight for civil rights and peace for the rest of his life. Although his work was cut short by tragedy, he accomplished many important things in his 39 years on Earth. His legacy of leadership lives on today.

More Work to Be Done

The passage of the Civil Rights Act and Voting Rights Act didn't mean racism and discrimination had ended. They were still powerful forces in American life, and Martin continued to speak out about these problems.

Although other leaders, such as Malcolm X, pushed for a more forceful response to racism, Martin still believed in nonviolence.

Martin focused on new causes too. He was against the war the United States was fighting in Vietnam in the 1960s. He also

Martin and Malcolm X both wanted to help Black people, but they had very different ideas about the best way to do that.

wanted to help people in poverty. He felt so strongly about it that he formed the Poor People's Campaign to fight for **economic justice**.

Murder in Memphis

In 1968, Martin traveled to Memphis, Tennessee, to stand with garbage workers who were going on strike. He spoke at a church there on April 3, telling the people gathered there, "Like anybody, I would like to live a long life … But I'm not concerned about that now." Some people at the church said it felt like he was saying goodbye.

The next day, while standing on a **balcony** at the Lorraine Motel, Martin was shot and killed. Riots then broke out in cities across the United States. Martin was gone, but he wouldn't be forgotten.

Fast Fact
James Earl Ray pled guilty to killing Martin, but he later said he didn't do it and a larger **conspiracy** was behind Martin's death. Martin's family still believes we don't know the whole story behind his death.

Martin's funeral was held in Atlanta. Civil rights leaders, movie stars, athletes, and more than 100,000 others came to pay their final respects.

Remembering Martin

Coretta Scott King opened the King Center in 1968 to help make sure her husband's legacy lived on. Today, the King Center is joined by many other reminders of Martin's life and work across the United States.

Streets and parks in cities and towns are named after Martin. In addition, he has an official national memorial in Washington, D.C. The Martin Luther King, Jr. Memorial opened in 2011. It features Martin's image carved into a large stone along with powerful words he once said. People from around the world visit this memorial, which was the first of its kind to honor an African American.

Fast Fact

The Martin Luther King, Jr. Memorial was officially opened during Barack Obama's presidency. Obama was the first African American president of the United States.

On one side of the Martin Luther King, Jr. Memorial are the words, "Out of the mountain of despair, a stone of hope." Martin spoke these words during his "I Have a Dream" speech.

ON THE BIG SCREEN

The civil rights movement may have been one of the turning points of the 20th century, but there aren't a lot of popular movies about this period. However, the 2014 movie *Selma* gained a lot of attention for showing movie **audiences** more about this important chapter of American history.

Director Ava DuVernay's movie tells the story of the marches from Selma to Montgomery. It features many of the people who played a part in those marches, including Martin Luther King Jr. In the movie, Martin was played by David Oyelowo. *Selma* was a big success. People enjoyed getting a closer look at the civil rights movement.

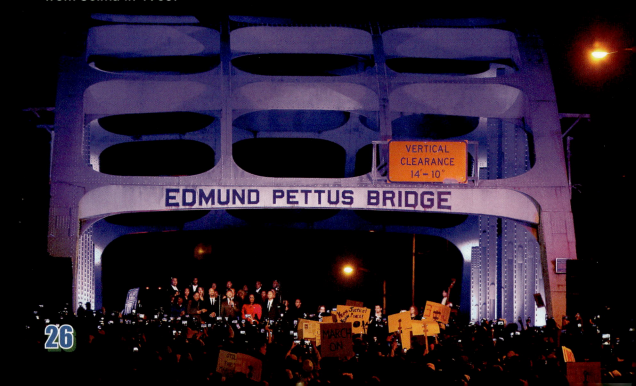

On Martin Luther King Jr. Day in 2015, some of the actors who starred in *Selma* walked across the Edmund Pettus Bridge to honor those who marched from Selma in 1965.

The Dream Lives On

Martin Luther King Jr. gave people hope. The night before he was killed, he said, "I've seen the Promised Land. I may not get there with you. But I want you to know tonight, that we, as a people, will get to the Promised Land." Martin saw huge changes made in the fight for equality during his lifetime, and he believed that even more would be made in the future.

Today, Martin's words still inspire people to keep fighting against racism. His dream lives on in the work of everyone who's trying to make the world a place where all people are treated equally.

Martin Luther King Jr. has inspired generations of protesters who speak out against injustice.

TIMELINE

In Martin's Life | In the World

1929
Martin Luther King Jr. is born on January 15.

1929
The U.S. stock market crashes, beginning the Great Depression.

1939–1945
World War II is fought.

1950
The Korean War begins.

1957
Martin helps start the Southern Christian Leadership Conference.

1963
Martin leads marches in Alabama and Washington, D.C.

1963
President John F. Kennedy is assassinated.

1965
Martin marches in Selma, and the Voting Rights Act passes.

1968
Martin is killed on April 4, and the King Center opens.

1969
Neil Armstrong becomes the first person to walk on the moon.

THINK ABOUT IT!

1. Why do you think Martin was chosen to lead the Montgomery bus boycott?

2. Why did some Black leaders disagree with Martin's methods?

3. Television played a big part in the civil rights movement. In what ways does technology continue to put the fight for civil rights in the spotlight?

4. Find a quote by Martin that inspires you. What quote is it? What do you like about it?

GLOSSARY

audience: A group of people who gather together to listen to or watch something.

balcony: A raised platform that is connected to the side of a building and is surrounded by a low wall or railing.

conspiracy: A secret agreement to do something harmful or illegal.

disturb: To make something disordered or upset.

dynamite: A powerful explosive often used in the form of a stick.

economic justice: The idea of creating a more fair and equal economy, in which everyone can make a living wage.

era: A period of time in history.

legacy: The lasting effect of a person or thing.

memorial: Something created to honor a person who has died.

role: A part, job, or function.

spokesperson: A man or woman who speaks for or represents something.

FIND OUT MORE

Books
Taylor-Butler, Christine. *Martin Luther King, Jr. Memorial*. New York, NY: Children's Press, 2019.

Vietze, Andrew. *The Life and Death of Martin Luther King Jr.* New York, NY: Rosen Publishing, 2018.

We Are Change: Words of Inspiration from Civil Rights Leaders. San Francisco, CA: Chronicle Books, 2019.

Websites
Hero for All: Martin Luther King, Jr.
kids.nationalgeographic.com/explore/history/martin-luther-king-jr/
This website features facts and a video about Martin's life.

King for Kids
kinginstitute.stanford.edu/king-kids
Visitors to this website will find primary sources related to Martin's life, a list of other books to read, and an animated version of the "I Have a Dream" speech.

Martin Luther King, Jr. Memorial
www.nps.gov/mlkm/index.htm
You can plan a trip to visit the Martin Luther King, Jr. Memorial with the help of the National Park Service.

Publisher's note to educators and parents: Our editors have carefully reviewed these websites to ensure that they are suitable for students. Many websites change frequently, however, and we cannot guarantee that a site's future contents will continue to meet our high standards of quality and educational value. Be advised that students should be closely supervised whenever they access the Internet.

INDEX

A
arrests, 12, 14
assassination, 8, 24, 28

B
Black Lives Matter, 9
"Bloody Sunday," 20
Boston University, 5, 11

C
Civil Rights Act of 1964, 21, 23

D
dynamite, 14

E
Ebenezer Baptist Church, 10
economic justice, 24
Edmund Pettus Bridge, 20, 26

I
"I Have a Dream" speech, 4, 5, 6, 18, 25

K
King Center, 8, 25, 28
King, Coretta Scott, 8, 11, 12, 25

L
"Letter from a Birmingham Jail," 17

M
March on Washington for Jobs and Freedom, 5, 18, 19, 28
Martin Luther King, Jr. Memorial, 22, 25
Montgomery bus boycott, 13, 14
Morehouse College, 11

N
Nobel Peace Prize, 19

O
Obama, Barack, 25

P
Parks, Rosa, 12, 13
Poor People's Campaign, 24
protests, 9, 13, 15, 17, 27

R
racism, 6, 7, 8, 9, 11, 13, 23, 27
Ray, James Earl, 24

S
segregation, 7, 11, 12, 13, 14, 17, 18, 21
Selma (movie), 26
Southern Christian Leadership Conference (SCLC), 14, 28

V
Voting Rights Act of 1965, 21, 23, 28

X
X, Malcolm, 23